American JAZZ

BENNY GOODMAN

JOANNE MATTERN

Mitchell Lane
PUBLISHERS
P.O. Box 196
Hockessin, Delaware 19707

American JAZZ

Benny Goodman

Bessie Smith

Billie Holiday

Charlie Parker

Count Basie

Dizzy Gillespie

Louis Armstrong

Miles Davis

Ornette Coleman

Scott Joplin

Printing   1   2   3   4   5   6   7   8   9

Library of Congress
Cataloging-in-Publication Data

Mattern, Joanne, 1963–
 Benny Goodman / by Joanne Mattern.
  p. cm. — (American jazz)
 Includes bibliographical references and index.
 ISBN 978-1-61228-269-5 (library bound)
 1. Goodman, Benny, 1909–1986—Juvenile literature. 2. Clarinetists—United States—Biography—Juvenile literature. 3. Jazz musicians—United States—Biography—Juvenile literature. I. Title.
 ML3930.G66M38 2013
 781.65092—dc23
 [B]
                                                2012008483

eBook ISBN: 9781612283456

PLB

Contents

Chapter 1

An Overnight Success?

Benny Goodman couldn't help feeling discouraged. His record company, MCA, had sent him and his band on a cross-country tour of the United States. The band traveled from city to city, usually playing just one night in each location before moving on to the next stop.

The trip wasn't easy. The pay was not great, even for 1935. Sometimes the band earned only two hundred and fifty dollars a night, which was split among all the members. There wasn't enough money for a bus, so band members drove their own cars from one city to the next. Singer Helen Ward remembers the long road trips. "Oh, those one-nighters," she told author Ross Firestone. "We were always hungry and tired, and the cars would break down in the middle of nowhere. And the distances we had to travel! I remember driving through one state after another to get to the next location."[1] Ward and her companions even made up a song about MCA and their travels, which they sang to the tune of the popular song "On the Road to Mandalay":

> On the road for MCA,
> Many places do we play.
> We're in Dallas, Texas, on a Wednesday.
> Thursday, York, PA.
> On the road for MCA . . .
> Where the dawn is waking
> We'll be breaking
> Our necks for MCA."[2]

Vocalist Helen Ward first joined Goodman's band for his radio show, Let's Dance. At that time, she was much better known than Goodman was.

Goodman and his bandmates might not have minded the rough schedule if they had been playing to bigger crowds. It wasn't as if no one had heard of Benny Goodman. He performed every week on a popular NBC radio program called *Let's Dance*. The show broadcast three bands with three different styles of music. Goodman's band played "hot" dance music in a popular new style known as swing. The show was broadcast all across the country and had many fans. However, it seemed that these fans weren't willing to come out and see Goodman perform. "I began to wonder what happened to all those radio listeners who'd written us fan letters," Goodman said.[3]

The low point came when the band reached Denver, Colorado. The band had been looking forward to this stop because they would be playing at a dance hall for three weeks and would enjoy a break from the constant traveling. But the gig turned into a disaster on the very first night. The club's manager complained that the band's music was too loud and was driving customers away. He demanded that Goodman play some slow waltzes and maybe dress his musicians in funny hats for comic effect. If they didn't, he threatened, he'd cancel the three-week engagement altogether.

Goodman was furious, but he knew he had to do something or the entire tour might be canceled. He worked up some slower dance arrangements, but the crowds and the manager still weren't happy. However, the band was allowed to play for the three-week engagement and the tour went on.

Goodman was devastated by the crowd's lack of interest in his hot swing music. He spent every day locked in his hotel room and even told people that he was going to give up the band. Band mates convinced him to keep going, and the tour headed west.

When the band pulled up in front of McFadden's Ballroom in Oakland, California, they were shocked to see a huge crowd of people waiting to get in. The police were even there to keep order. Goodman could not believe all those people were there to see his band. He was sure that the crowd had confused him with another band and that they had arrived on the wrong night.

Finally, it was showtime. The theater manager opened the door and the crowd surged in. Instead of sitting back and waiting to dance, everyone rushed right up to the bandstand. Goodman still thought the crowd was there to see someone else, but he decided that if he had made a mistake, he might as well go all out. He called for the band to play "King Porter Stomp," one of their liveliest tunes. To his amazement, the crowd started yelling and stomping. "I thought a riot had broken out," Goodman recalled to Firestone. "Finally the truth got through to me. We were causing the riot. What was even more amazing, the fans seemed to get wilder and wilder as the night wore on. I was positive it was a fluke, and that we'd just had the good luck to be booked into a jazz-mad town."[4]

It seemed Goodman was right. Their next few gigs were awful, including one in a smelly barn that was used to store fish and another where patrons threw bottles at them. By the time the band reached Los Angeles on August 21 to play at the famous Palomar Ballroom, Goodman was once again sure that his career as a bandleader was over.

That night something happened that would change his mind forever.

Goodman began the show playing his sweetest, most commercial arrangements. The crowd was polite, but they clearly weren't very excited. Then one of Goodman's sidemen suggested that they might as well go down swinging. Goodman agreed, and the band jumped into some of their liveliest music.

The crowd's response changed immediately. Instead of dancing, they rushed up to the bandstand, just as they had in Oakland. These people weren't there to dance. They were there to swing! "That was the moment that decided things for me," Goodman explained forty years later in an interview celebrating the Palomar concert. "After traveling three thousand miles, we finally found people who were up on what we were trying to do, prepared to take our music the way we wanted to play it. That first big roar from the crowd was one of the sweetest sounds I ever heard in my life, and from that time on the night kept getting bigger and bigger, as we played about every good number in our book."[5]

No one was really sure why the crowds in Los Angeles and Oakland were so excited about Goodman's music and why he received such a different reception in other parts of the country. One explanation was that the Let's Dance radio program was broadcast very late in New York but aired earlier in California because of the time difference, so the show had a larger audience on the West Coast. Another reason was that a Los Angeles disc jockey named Al Jarvis liked Goodman's music and had been playing him regularly on his show. The West Coast audience also may have been more familiar with big band jazz because other musicians, such as Louis Armstrong, had toured there before Benny Goodman came to town.

Whatever the reason, the performance at the Palomar changed Goodman's life forever. It also changed American music. Some people say that the Swing Era was born that night, although other bands had been playing swing music before Goodman became famous. Something amazing happened that night, something magical, and it wasn't long before Benny Goodman was a household name all across the nation. "The King of Swing" had arrived.

The Golden Age of Radio

Before television was widely available, radio provided the most common and popular form of entertainment to people around the world. Radios first came into use in 1921, and by 1935, more than 22 million homes had radio receivers. Radios of that time were not the small units we have today but were large, elegant pieces of furniture that were often the most important pieces in a room. Family and friends would gather around and listen to the radio, using their imagination to visualize what they heard through the speakers.

At first, individual stations came up with their own programming, but this was expensive and it was hard to find high-quality actors and production crews. During the late 1930s, radio networks came into being. Networks allowed stations to band together and share the cost of programming. This made a greater variety of high-quality programming available to families all across the United States. Radio networks produced all types of entertainment, including musical programs, soap operas, mysteries, crime dramas, science fiction, comedies, westerns, and news. Most historians consider the 1930s and 1940s to be the Golden Age of Radio. During the 1930s, America was struggling through the Great Depression, and people were looking for cheap forms of entertainment. A radio could provide hours of imaginative fun for the entire family.

Chapter **2**

Hard Times

Benjamin David Goodman was born on May 30, 1909, in Chicago, Illinois. His parents were David Goodman and Dora Grisinsky Goodman. David Goodman was born in Warsaw, Poland, which was then under Russian control. Dora was born in Kaunas, Lithuania. Both of them had immigrated to the United States to escape persecution because they were Jewish. The couple met in Baltimore, Maryland, in the early 1890s, where they married and quickly started a family. In 1903, the Goodmans moved to Chicago.

Benny was one of a crowd. He was the ninth of twelve children in the Goodman family. The family was desperately poor and lived in a tiny apartment in a tenement in the Maxwell Street neighborhood. The Goodmans moved frequently when Benny was growing up, often because they didn't have enough money to pay the rent.

David Goodman had been a tailor in Warsaw, but he was unable to make a steady living in that field in the United States. Instead, he worked at a variety of jobs, usually working twelve to fourteen hours a day, six days a week. Benny had vivid memories of his father working in Chicago's stockyards, where animals were slaughtered for food and other products. The job was disgusting and exhausting, and it hurt Benny to think of his father having to do that all day. In 1956, he told *DownBeat* magazine, "He'd come home at the end of the day exhausted, stinking to high heaven, and when he walked in it made me sick. I couldn't stand it.

I couldn't stand the idea of Pop every day standing in that stuff, shoveling it around."[1]

Even in the best of times, David Goodman didn't earn more than a few dollars a week. Dora Goodman, who never learned how to read or write and spoke very poor English, had too many children to raise to find any paying work, and in fact, she often did not leave the apartment for weeks at a time because the children kept her so busy. When Benny was born, his oldest siblings were teenagers. They were able to find jobs and add a small amount of money to the family income. Still, life was hard. Benny later recalled, "I can remember when we lived in a basement without heat during the winter, and a couple of times when there wasn't anything to eat. I don't mean *much* to eat. I mean *anything.* This isn't an experience you forget in a hurry. I haven't ever forgotten it."[2] Benny's childhood was so unhappy that he barely spoke about it when he was older, telling interviewers that he preferred to block out most of his memories of that time.

Despite his hard life, David Goodman did his best for his large family. He insisted that his children study hard and do well in school so that they would have a better chance in life. "Pop was always trying to get us to study, so that we would get ahead in the world," Benny later wrote. "He always envied people with book-learning and education. Whatever any of us have amounted to may be pretty much traced to him."[3]

Music provided one of the few bright spots in the Goodman family's harsh life. David Goodman would bring his children to free band concerts in the park on Sunday afternoons. When Benny was about ten years old, David found out that his neighbor's children earned a little bit of money playing musical instruments at local parties and other events. Immediately, David had an idea. Perhaps playing music was a way his children could make a better life for themselves.

Soon afterward, David Goodman discovered that a local synagogue provided free instruments and charged only twenty-five cents for music lessons for boys. He immediately signed up Benny and his brothers Freddy and Harry. The boys were given instruments based on their size. While his older brothers got trumpets and trombones, little Benny got a smaller instrument, the clarinet. The boys went to the synagogue for lessons several times a week, walking a mile in each direction. They often walked to the home of their teacher, an elderly man named Moissaye Boguslawski, for additional lessons as well.

After a year, the synagogue ran out of money and ended the music program. The boys' lessons with Mr. Boguslawski ended at that time too. However, David Goodman still wanted his boys to continue their musical education, and the boys were happy to do so. They joined the boys' band at Hull House, a famous settlement house founded by social activist Jane Addams. The band was one of Hull House's efforts to take poor boys off the street and give them an alternative to crime and violence. David Goodman was thrilled to provide this opportunity to his boys and sent them to Hull

Moissaye Boguslawski began playing at weddings when he was ten years old and often played piano in dance halls for eight to ten hours a day as a teen. He went on to perform with many U.S. orchestras and was a well-known professor and writer.

House for lessons. During the winter, he even pulled the boys through the snowy streets on a sled over the several-mile journey to Hull House.

At Hull House, the boys learned marching songs and upbeat classical music. The band members wore uniforms and performed at neighborhood parades, church picnics, and other local events. Jazz was not part of the program, but that didn't mean that the Goodman boys didn't hear it. One of their older brothers bought a record player and some jazz records for the family to enjoy in their apartment. The boys also heard jazz music at the movies and local concerts. Benny's brother

Freddy recalled a time when Benny got so excited by the music at a concert that he jumped up on stage, grabbed the instrument from the clarinet player, and started to play. He also copied the clarinet solos from records and played them back, note for note. Everyone agreed that Benny was a natural musician.

Around this time, Benny began taking private lessons with a German clarinetist named Franz Schoepp. Schoepp was a well-known musician who trained clarinetists from the Chicago Symphony. No one is sure how a young boy like Benny managed to arrange lessons with such a famous teacher, but it is likely that Schoepp had some connection with Hull House and was told about the clarinet prodigy playing there.

Benny's private lessons cost fifty cents a week, which was a stretch for the family budget, but they were worth every penny. Schoepp was a demanding teacher who insisted that his students learn the correct way to play. He gave Benny a strong foundation and taught him all the correct techniques of fingering and breathing, and the proper mouth position, or embouchure. Schoepp's training set Benny apart from many other jazz musicians of his day, who were often self-taught and picked up bad habits. Schoepp also gave Benny an attitude that music was important and should be taken seriously. Benny would take this lesson to heart. He often criticized his band members if they did not practice and perform perfectly.

Schoepp taught Benny one other important lesson: It was the musician who was important, not his race or religion. Schoepp was German at a time when many Germans persecuted Jews, yet he taught Benny and his other Jewish students the same way he taught everyone else. Schoepp also had African-American students, which was unheard of in a time when prejudice and segregation were the normal way of life in the United States. Benny came to know several African-American clarinetists at Schoepp's house, and he learned a lot from them. He was impressed by Schoepp's attitude. Later, when Benny led his own band, he did not hesitate to work with African-American musicians, a decision that changed swing music forever.

Hull House

Social activists Jane Addams and Ellen Gates Starr started Hull House in 1889. The two women got the idea after visiting a similar organization, called a settlement house, in England. At that time, Chicago's neighborhoods were packed with immigrant families from Europe. Hull House's clients included Italians, Greeks, Mexicans, Scandinavians, Poles, Germans, Russians, Czechoslovakians, French families, Lithuanians, Hungarians, Rumanians, Yugoslavians, and Belgians. Many of these families were desperately poor and lived under very difficult conditions. Addams and Starr wanted to create a place where immigrants could learn a trade, study English, eat nutritious meals, and find jobs. Hull House also ran a preschool and kindergarten for children who were too young to attend public school. It hosted concerts and art shows, which allowed immigrants to share and take pride in their cultural heritage.

By 1907, Hull House had grown to include thirteen buildings spread over a large city block. Most of the organization's funding came from donations, and Hull House was lucky enough to have the support of many wealthy philanthropists (people who give money to charity). Although the huge wave of immigrants had pretty much ended by the 1920s, Hull House continued  to serve the poor people of Chicago until it closed in 1963. After that, the original Hull House served as a museum.

chapter 3

"The Kid in Short Pants"

Benny's old music teacher, Mr. Boguslawski, remained part of his life even after their lessons ended. His son, Ziggy Boguslawski, was the director of the Central Park Theater's vaudeville house. One night, Benny went over to the theater on Amateur Night, which was a chance for anyone to get up onstage and perform. Because he was so young, Benny was not allowed on the stage, so instead he stood on the conductor's podium in the orchestra pit and played from there. The little boy made a big impression on Ziggy Boguslawski.

Benny continued to study and perform for the next few years. He was so focused on practicing and playing clarinet that his mother would throw him out of the apartment with instructions to play outside.

When Benny was twelve years old, Ziggy needed someone to fill in for an act that had canceled at the theater. He sent for Benny and told him to get his clarinet and hurry over to the theater. With barely any rehearsal, Benny played several songs with the band. The audience loved it. Even though he was not even a teenager, Benny was not at all nervous to be performing with the band. "The applause was nice," he later said, "but the five bucks they paid me was even better, because it was the first money I ever earned playing clarinet."[1]

In 1922, Benny graduated from Sheppard Grammar School and moved on to Harrison High. There he met a number of other jazz musicians. The group became known as the Austin High Gang and included many other young men who would go on to become well-known swing and jazz musicians. One of them, Jimmy McPartland, often played at parties at local universities. Although Benny was several years younger, McPartland often hired him to play clarinet. McPartland was impressed by Benny's talent at improvisation, which was rare in that day and age. Sometimes Benny worked three or four nights a week, making ten or fifteen dollars each time. That was a lot of money, especially for a boy who had just entered his teens. He became known as the Kid in Short Pants because he still wore the short pants that were the fashion for young boys of that era.

By the time he was fourteen, Benny realized that he could not go to school and still be a professional musician, so he left Harrison High and started his full-time music career. After playing with several bands and appearing at many local dance halls around Chicago, Benny met a drummer named Ben Pollack. Pollack was originally from Chicago but had gone on to lead a band in Los Angeles. He invited Benny, who was only sixteen, to join his band. Benny said yes and headed to California.

Ben Pollack and His Orchestra opened a new world to Goodman. Pollack had started playing "hot jazz" with musicians from New Orleans in a style known as Dixieland. Hot jazz was faster and livelier than traditional jazz, and it was exactly the sound Pollack wanted when he started his own orchestra. Goodman was a great fit for Pollack's band. Pollack loved Goodman's ability to improvise as well as the fact that Goodman could read music and play arrangements without much study. Pollack's band also featured several soloists, and it was common for Goodman and the other members of the band to take turns playing long, improvised solos during concerts. For Goodman, this was an amazingly free and exciting way to express himself through music.

Goodman was enjoying his time with the Ben Pollack Orchestra. However, he had been in the band for only a short time when tragedy struck. His father stepped off a streetcar and was hit by a car. David was severely injured and died the next day without ever waking up. For Benny, the loss of his beloved father was devastating. Now that Goodman

Ben Pollack sits in front of his orchestra, with Goodman standing behind him in the center of the first row. Pollack was one of the most popular bandleaders of the 1920s. He allowed his band members the freedom to play solos and shape the music to their own taste.

had a steady job and was making good money, he had wanted his father to quit working and enjoy life. However, David Goodman told his son, "You take care of yourself, I'll take care of myself,"[2] and refused to let Benny support him. Soon afterward, David was killed. Benny was troubled for the rest of his life that his father had died before Benny achieved the tremendous fame that was soon to come.

In 1928, Pollack received an offer to move his orchestra to New York City to play at a well-known hotspot called the Little Club. Pollack jumped at the chance. Although Chicago had been the center of the jazz world in the early 1920s, by the end of the decade, the hottest scene had moved to New York. Many musicians traveled east to be part of the new scene, and Pollack was quick to follow. Goodman went along for the ride. He would be based in New York City for the rest of his life.

Pollack's band played in several clubs around New York. Goodman also played on radio shows. In 1926 he made his first recording with Ben Pollack and His Orchestra. In 1928, Goodman made his first solo record, called *Clarinettis,* for Vocalion Records.

By then, Goodman was earning up to six hundred fifty dollars a week and had plenty of work. In addition to performing at dance halls and on the radio, he and Pollack's band were the orchestra for a new Broadway show called *Hello, Daddy.* Up to that point, Pollack had stayed behind the scenes in his band, performing as the drummer. When the band moved to Broadway, he decided to step out from behind the drums and become a true bandleader. This change did not sit well with Goodman and some of the other musicians. In those days, bandleaders controlled every aspect of the musicians' lives, including how they dressed and how they spent their free time. Pollack's band was not happy that someone who had been "one of the guys" was suddenly bossing them around.

Goodman's old friend Jimmy McPartland quit the band after Pollack yelled at him for playing handball between shows and then going onstage in dirty, scuffed shoes. Goodman quit at the same time. Pollack was not sorry to see Goodman go, complaining, "Benny Goodman was getting in everybody's hair about this time, because he was getting good and took all the choruses"[3] (meaning he was showing off and playing more solos than other members).

For the next few years, Goodman played at clubs around New York City and continued to perform on the radio and make jazz recordings. He played with some of swing's up-and-coming stars, including Glenn Miller, Bob Crosby, Gene Krupa, Tommy and Jimmy Dorsey, and Jack Teagarden. Then, in 1933, Goodman met a man who would help push his career to the highest ranks of fame.

Dixieland Jazz

Dixieland jazz began in the late teens and early 1920s in New Orleans, Louisiana. It most likely got its name from a New Orleans group called the Original Dixieland jazz band, who made the first publicly available recording of this style of music in 1917. "Dixie" was also a nickname for the South during the Civil War. Other names for Dixieland jazz are New Orleans jazz or traditional jazz. Early Dixieland jazz bands combined old French marching tunes with a type of lively music called ragtime.

Dixieland bands usually include a trumpet, clarinet, trombone, saxophone, banjo, drums, piano, string bass, and tuba. This type of music was usually completely instrumental, so bands did not have singers. Dixieland jazz has a steady, fast beat with a swinging rhythm. Often the tuba and string bass play on the first and third beats of each measure while the banjo and piano play on the second and fourth beats. Meanwhile, the other instruments play melodies and countermelodies that keep the music moving along.

Trumpet player Louis Armstrong was perhaps the most famous Dixieland jazz musician. Other popular Dixieland jazz musicians were pianist Jelly Roll Morton, trumpeter Bix Beiderbecke, clarinetist Sidney

Bechet, and trumpet player and bandleader King Oliver. Dixieland songs such as "When the Saints Go Marchin' In" and "Basin Street Blues" are still popular.

Chapter 4

A Rocket Ride to Fame

In 1933, Goodman met a jazz fan named John Hammond. Like Goodman, Hammond became interested in jazz at a young age, but unlike Goodman, he came from a wealthy family. Throughout his teens and early twenties, he spent a lot of time in the New York neighborhood of Harlem, which was the center of the blues and jazz scene in the city. Hammond later got a job as a writer for a music magazine and began a quest to find the best jazz musicians and sign them to record deals. By the time he met Goodman, Hammond had become one of the most influential figures in jazz music.

That year, Hammond received a contract from the British branch of Columbia Records to make several "sides," or records. He knew about Goodman, of course, and hired him to record four sides. The two soon became good friends, although Hammond was a demanding producer who did everything from picking the songs to deciding who would play them. Goodman was just as strong a presence, however, and the two ended up compromising on the musicians and the style of music. The records were successful enough in Britain that they were released in the United States, and Goodman was signed to an American record contract with Columbia.

By 1934, Benny Goodman had made almost 500 records for a variety of companies and under a variety of band names. He was ready to form a band of his own and be a true bandleader. Goodman did not like

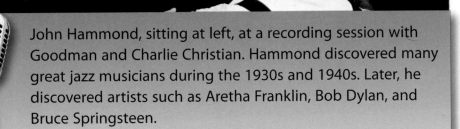

John Hammond, sitting at left, at a recording session with Goodman and Charlie Christian. Hammond discovered many great jazz musicians during the 1930s and 1940s. Later, he discovered artists such as Aretha Franklin, Bob Dylan, and Bruce Springsteen.

taking orders from other musicians and decided it was time for him to be his own boss. Many musicians were eager to play with him, since he had such a good reputation as a hot jazz performer with great improvisation skills. Goodman soon had his big band and was performing around New York City.

Before the year was out, Goodman and his band auditioned for an NBC radio program called *Let's Dance.* The program featured three bands playing various styles of dance music, including sweet dance music that was very commercial, Latin music, and a style of hot jazz that was being called by a new name: swing. Goodman quickly landed the "hot" part of the program. He performed weekly on *Let's Dance* until May 1935, when

Fletcher Henderson's smooth jazz sound made him one of the most popular bandleaders of the 1920s and helped bring about the swing style of music in the 1930s. Henderson later became the first African-American musician to join Goodman's band.

a strike shut down the program. The show gave people all over the United States their first chance to hear Goodman and his lively music.

John Hammond helped by suggesting that Goodman purchase hot swing arrangements from Fletcher Henderson, a popular African-American musician who led one of New York City's most popular African-American big bands of the time. This turned out to be a great idea for both Goodman and Henderson. Goodman's support helped Henderson financially. It also helped many of Henderson's band members, who were paid to teach Goodman's musicians how to play the music.

After *Let's Dance* went off the air, Goodman took his band on their cross-country tour of the United States, which ended with their electrifying performance at the Palomar Ballroom in Los Angeles. That night is sometimes called the beginning of the Swing Era. However, as writer Donald Clarke pointed out, "It is clear in retrospect that the Swing Era had been waiting to happen, but it was Goodman and his band that touched it off."[1]

By 1937, Benny Goodman was known as the King of Swing, a nickname given to him by magazine writers. Later that year, his publicist suggested that Goodman and his band perform at Carnegie Hall in New York City. Carnegie Hall was world-famous for classical music performances. Goodman would be the first jazz bandleader to perform at this legendary concert hall.

At first, Goodman was unsure about the idea. "When the thing was first put up to me I was a little dubious about it, not knowing just what would be expected of us," he said. "But as soon as it was understood that we could handle things in our own way, and let the people listen to it as they would any other kind of music, the proposition really began to mean something."[2]

The concert was held on January 16, 1938. Tickets sold out weeks before the event. Goodman began with three of the band's most recent tunes, "Don't Be That Way," "Sometimes I'm Happy," and "One O'Clock Jump." After a set that included a history of jazz from its Dixieland roots, the band moved into a jam session, followed by more of the band's popular numbers, including solos by various band members and guests. The band closed with the classic "Sing, Sing, Sing," a rowdy piece that featured solos from many of the band's members, including drummer Gene Krupa. The audience went wild.

History was made that night at Carnegie Hall. For the first time, jazz was performed for and accepted by a mainstream audience. The evening was one of the most significant in jazz history. Goodman was thrilled with the performance. He said, "That night at Carnegie Hall was a great experience. . . . It was the thrill of my life to walk out on that stage with people just hemming the band in and hear the greeting the guys got."[3] The concert was recorded and became one of the best-selling live jazz albums of all time. It is still in print today.

Goodman's popularity continued to soar. The structure of his band changed over the years, from a big band to a trio, then a quartet, and then a sextet. He played with a number of swing's best musicians, although many agreed he was not the easiest man to work with. Goodman expected perfection from himself and demanded the same from everyone who worked with him. Many musicians spoke about "the ray," a frosty glare that Goodman gave any musician who failed to meet his high standards. He once got so angry at his guitarist that he sent the musician all the way to the back of the bandstand where no one could hear him. Some of his band members actively disliked him. Singer Helen Forrest once said, "The twenty or so months I spent with Benny felt like twenty years. They seem like a life sentence."[4]

Goodman also had a reputation as being arrogant and conceited. As biographer James Lincoln Collier notes, "Throughout his life he frequently failed to show any concern for the people around him who were—or should have been—important to him. He was constantly hurting people by making remarks the effects of which he seems to have been totally unaware."[5] Perhaps Goodman was too focused on music to care much about people, or perhaps his focus was on himself rather than the world around him. Whatever the reason, many people found Goodman hard to get along with.

Although many band members considered Goodman to be tight-fisted and cheap, others recall acts of generosity. Trumpet player Jimmy Maxwell described how Goodman once refused to lend him five hundred dollars so Maxwell's sister could have an operation, but a few weeks later he gave Maxwell three hundred and fifty dollars after his wallet, containing his entire paycheck, was stolen. Goodman also gave Maxwell a thousand dollars to live on while he was out of work, and he invited Maxwell to stay at his house in the country while Maxwell recovered from a serious illness. Goodman also kept paying several of his musicians while they were in the hospital and unable to work. He secretly gave scholarships to students in music schools.

Goodman also had strong ideas about integration. During the 1930s and 1940s, most bands were either all white or all black because clubs

Along with his own compositions, Goodman also popularized classic American tunes by others, including "Blue Skies" by Irving Berlin and "I Got Rhythm" by George and Ira Gershwin.

Goodman plays the clarinet on the steps of Capitol Hill on St. Patrick's Day, 1939. He is accompanied by Senator Joseph O'Mahoney on harp, at left. Senator Claude Pepper is seated on the steps, and Eunice Healy, a dancer in Goodman's show, stands above them.

Goodman, with actor Jack Oakie, appeared as himself in the 1944 movie *Sweet and Low-Down*. Although the plot was not very good, the movie is known for the amazing musical performances of Goodman and his band.

and concert halls refused to allow different races to perform together. In the Southern states, it was actually against the law to do so. Goodman refused to follow these traditions and became one of the first major bandleaders to hire African-American musicians. During the 1930s, he hired African-American pianist Teddy Wilson, vibraphonist Lionel Hampton, and guitarist Charlie Christian. Talent was what mattered to Goodman, not skin color. "If a guy's got it, let him give it," he once said. "I'm selling music, not prejudice."[6]

Mel Powell, a pianist and arranger for the Goodman band, explained, "Benny was one of the very, very few white people I've known who had not a fiber of racism in him. He was absolutely, authentically color-blind, and he thought all the fuss kicked up by the press whenever he hired a black musician was silly." Referring to Goodman's reputation as difficult to get along with, Powell added, "One of the real giveaways to his outlook was that he could be as rude to a black man as to a white man."[7]

Leading an integrated band was sometimes problematic. Goodman's bands could not tour in the Deep South because of the racist laws there. Even in the North, there were problems. Goodman was quick to stand up for his musicians if there was trouble. When someone once referred to Teddy Wilson using a derogatory racial term, Goodman replied, "I'll knock you out if you use that word around me again."[8] And if Goodman ever heard that his African-American band members were having problems at a concert hall or club, he would threaten to walk out—and take the entire band with him.

Goodman's popularity continued to soar, but music styles began to change in the late 1940s. His career was about to take a new direction.

Big Bands and Big Bandleaders

Big bands really were big. They were more of an orchestra in terms of size and not the smaller bands we think of today. A big band usually included fifteen to twenty musicians. It might have three to five trumpets, two to four trombones, plus saxophones, clarinets, flutes, a piano, guitar, bass, and drums, and one or two vocalists (often a male and a female). Other instruments might be added as well, depending on the band and bandleader. All those instruments created the big, swinging sound that was the trademark of this style of music.

Bandleaders had a lot of responsibility. A bandleader not only picked the musicians he wanted to work with, he was also responsible for choosing the music and arranging it (or hiring an arranger) so that his band could play it. It was up to the bandleader to lead rehearsals and performances. He set the tempo, adjusted the volume, assigned solos, and called out what song would be played next. Each concert might be different than the one before, since each audience responded to the music in a different way. It was up to the bandleader to sense what each audience wanted and then direct the band to play the songs and the style that pleased the crowd the most.

The King of Swing and big bandleader, Benny Goodman

Beyond Swing

Music was changing by the mid-1940s. Swing was no longer the most popular style of jazz. Instead, new forms such as bebop and a style known as cool jazz became popular. Goodman was happy to experiment with this new form, and he put together a bebop band around 1945. He enjoyed his band at first, but his heart was really with swing music.

After a year and a half, he re-formed the band and went back to playing swing arrangements. He later complained about bebop: "Basically, it's all wrong. It's not even knowing the scales."[1] Also during the 1940s, vocalists such as Frank Sinatra became extremely popular with teen audiences, leading to a change in music that saw singers become more important than instrumentalists.

Goodman had trained with classical musicians during his youth, and he returned to that style of music during the 1940s, after giving up bebop. During the 1940s and 1950s, he frequently played with top classical clarinetists. In 1949, he began studying with Reginald Kell, one of the world's leading classical clarinetists.

Studying classical music after playing jazz music for so long wasn't easy. Goodman had to change his embouchure. Instead of holding the clarinet's mouthpiece between his front teeth and lower lip, he learned to use both lips. He also learned new fingering techniques. He went on to play with symphony orchestras, and also premiered classical works by

Goodman, at right, performs with his bebop band (from left: Francis Beecher, Clyde Lombardi, Wardell Gray, and Sonny Igoe) at New York City's legendary Stork Club in 1948.

such major twentieth-century composers as Béla Bartók, Leonard Bernstein, and Igor Stravinsky.

Goodman was not finished with jazz, however. In 1953, his friend John Hammond arranged a tour with Louis Armstrong's All-Stars. Goodman re-formed his band for the tour, but unfortunately the result was a disaster. The two bandleaders did not get along, and Goodman was horrified at Armstrong's act, which included comedy and even one female singer doing splits onstage. Music historian Donald Clarke called the act, "a contradiction of everything Goodman stood for."[2] The tour ended almost before it began.

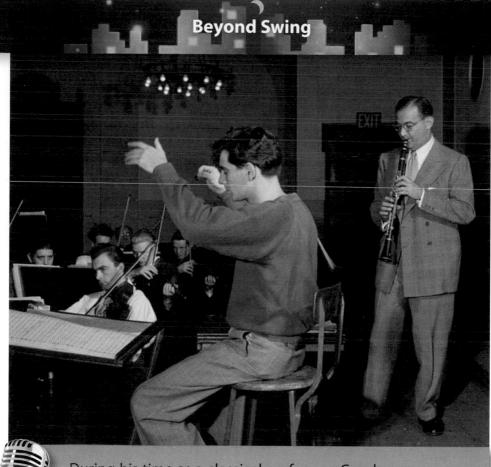

During his time as a classical performer, Goodman performed a concert with legendary conductor and composer Leonard Bernstein at Carnegie Hall in New York City. Bernstein was one of the towering figures of twentieth-century classical music.

A movie about Goodman's life, *The Benny Goodman Story,* appeared in 1955. The movie starred Steve Allen as Goodman and was heavily fictionalized, but it introduced Goodman's music to a new audience and reunited him with some of his old band mates, including Ben Pollack, Gene Krupa, and Lionel Hampton.

Goodman also brought his music to fans around the world. During the winter of 1956–1957, he and his band went on a sold-out tour of Asia. During this trip, he was able to jam with Thailand's king, Bhumibol Adulyadej. In 1958 and 1959, Goodman brought his band to Western Europe, touring Belgium and several other countries.

The story of A FABULOUS GUY A WONDERFUL GIRL and the EXCITING MUSIC they made together!

the Benny Goodman Story

A Universal-International Picture starring

STEVE ALLEN
DONNA REED

COLOR BY TECHNICOLOR

All the great Goodman HITS including: "SING, SING, SING" · "STOMPIN' AT THE SAVOY" · "BUGLE CALL RAG" · "ONE O'CLOCK JUMP" · "LET'S DANCE" · "AVALON"

with GENE KRUPA · LIONEL HAMPTON · BEN POLLACK · TEDDY WILSON · EDWARD "KID" ORY
and Guest Stars HARRY JAMES · MARTHA TILTON · ZIGGY ELMAN and the incomparable BENNY GOODMAN playing the Cl

Written and Directed by VALENTINE DAVIES · Produced by AARON ROSENBERG

For a long time, Goodman had wanted to perform in the Soviet Union. This did not seem possible because the Soviet Union's communist government had outlawed jazz, calling it a product of decadent American culture. However, the American and Soviet governments arranged a cultural exchange, and in 1962, Goodman and his band went on a swing concert tour of the Soviet Union. They played thirty-two concerts, which were attended by more than 180,000 Russians, including Soviet Premier (president) Nikita Khrushchev. One Soviet newspaper praised Goodman as a "true poet of the clarinet."[3]

Goodman's personal life also flourished. Through his friendship with John Hammond, Goodman met Hammond's sister, Alice. The couple married in 1942 and had two daughters, Benjie and Rachel. The family lived in the New York City suburbs until Alice's death in 1978.

Goodman continued to perform throughout the 1960s, 1970s, and 1980s. He appeared on many television specials, including a 1975 PBS salute to John Hammond. Goodman also continued to record and

Goodman delights jazz fans in Moscow's Red Square. The Soviet Union had banned jazz for many years before inviting Goodman and other musicians to perform there in 1962.

perform. In the 1970s, he collaborated with jazz guitarist George Benson to re-create some of the famous Benny Goodman and Charlie Christian duets from the 1930s.

In 1982, Goodman received one of the United States' highest awards when he was honored for his contributions in swing music at the Kennedy Center in Washington, D.C. In 1986, he received a Grammy Lifetime Achievement Award. Goodman was also named to the DownBeat

Benny Goodman with his wife, Alice, and their daughters, Rachel and Benjie

Jazz Hall of Fame in 1957 and to the National Association of Broadcasters Hall of Fame in the radio division in 1983.

Goodman continued to perform almost until his death, although his health was poor for many years. He died of a heart attack in his New York City home on June 13, 1986. He was seventy-seven years old. His musical papers and other items, including many never-before-heard recordings and rare photos, were donated to Yale University Library in New Haven, Connecticut, where they could be studied and preserved for years to come.

Benny Goodman is still known as the King of Swing and is still popular as a legendary bandleader and clarinetist. His dedication to jazz music and technical correctness made him one of the most important figures in music and an inspiration to other musicians.

Goodman's advice to Glenn Miller, another swing musician who would go on to lead a very successful big band of his own, gives a good idea of why this talented musician went so far. "I remember Glenn Miller coming to me once, before he had his own band, saying, 'How do you do it? How do you get started? It's so difficult.' I told him, 'I don't know but whatever you do, don't stop. Just keep on going. Because one way or the other, if you want to find reasons why you shouldn't keep on, you'll find 'em. The obstacles are all there; there are a million of 'em. But if you want to do something, you do it anyway, and handle the obstacles as they come."[4] Benny Goodman overcame every obstacle life placed in his way and created beautiful music for everyone to enjoy.

What Is Bebop?

Bebop is a very different type of jazz than swing. Instead of a large orchestra of fifteen to twenty people, a bebop group usually had only four to six players. The smaller size provided more opportunities for solos. The style of the music was also unlike anything heard in swing. Bebop music is characterized by more complicated melodies and chord progressions. There is also more emphasis on the rhythm section (drums and bass) instead of on the wind and brass instruments of a big band. The phrases in bebop music also do not follow a set rhythm the way swing music does. Instead, the length of the phrases is often irregular and changes frequently. This style makes bebop interesting to listen to, but very hard to dance to!

Bebop first became popular during the 1940s. Jazz musicians often gathered at two New York City clubs, Monroe's Uptown House and Minton's Playhouse, to jam and experiment with new ideas. Their jams were the roots of this new style of jazz.

Bebop got its unusual name from a nonsense syllable commonly used in scat singing. Scat singing uses improvised nonsense syllables sung to a melody that is also improvised. The development of bebop is attributed in large part to trumpeter Dizzy Gillespie and

Charlie Parker and Dizzy Gillespie

saxophonist Charlie Parker. Gillespie and Parker experimented with unconventional chord progressions, discordant sounds, and the unusual placement of accents in melodies.

1909	Benjamin David Goodman is born on May 30 in Chicago, Illinois.
1921	Benny fills in at a performance at Central Park Theater's vaudeville house.
1922	Benny graduates from Sheppard Grammar School. At Harrison High, he forms the Austin High Gang with Jimmy McPartland and other jazz musicians.
1923	Benny leaves school to become a full-time musician.
1925	He joins Ben Pollack and His Orchestra; they head to California.
1928	With Ben Pollack and His Orchestra, Goodman moves to New York City. He makes his first solo record, *Clarinettis*.
1929	He plays with Ben Pollack and His Orchestra in the Broadway musical *Hello, Daddy*. Goodman quits Pollack's band and goes solo.
1933	Goodman meets John Hammond.
1934	He auditions for *Let's Dance,* and performs on the show weekly until May 1935.
1935	At the Palomar Ballroom in Los Angeles on August 21, Goodman's performance gives birth to the Swing Era.
1938	Goodman and his band perform at New York's Carnegie Hall on January 16, the first time jazz is played for a mainstream audience.
1942	Benny marries Alice Hammond, John Hammond's sister.
1945	Goodman puts together a bebop band.
1949	He begins studying classical clarinet with Reginald Kell.
1953	Goodman tours with Louis Armstrong and The All-Stars.
1955	The movie *The Benny Goodman Story* premieres.
1956–1957	Goodman and his band tour Asia.
1957	Goodman is named to the DownBeat Jazz Hall of Fame.
1958–1959	Goodman and his band tour Europe.
1962	They play 32 swing concerts in a tour of the Soviet Union—where jazz had once been outlawed.
1978	Alice Goodman dies.
1982	Benny Goodman receives Kennedy Center Honors.
1983	He is named to the National Association of Broadcasters Hall of Fame.
1986	He dies of a heart attack in New York City on June 13.

Benny Goodman played on hundreds of albums and it is impossible to list them all here. This discography includes the most popular and important recordings of his career.

1928 *A Jazz Holiday*
1929 *Benny Goodman and the Giants of Swing*
       BG and Big Tea in NYC
1934 *Swinging '34, Vol. 1*
       Swinging '34, Vol. 2
1935 *Sing, Sing, Sing*
       The Birth of Swing
       Original Benny Goodman Trio and Quartet Sessions, Vol. 1:
              After You've Gone
       Stomping at the Savoy
1936 *Air Play Doctor*
1937 *Roll 'Em, Vol. 1*
       Roll 'Em, Vol. 2
1938 *From Spirituals to Swing*
       Carnegie Hall Concert Live (1938)
       Carnegie Hall Concert, Vol. 1 (Live)
       Carnegie Hall Concert, Vol. 2 (Live)
       Carnegie Hall Concert, Vol. 3 (Live)
1939 *Ciribiribin (Live)*
       Swingin' Down the Lane (Live)
       Featuring Charlie Christian
1940 *Eddie Sauter Arrangements*
1941 *Swing Into Spring*
1947 *Undercurrent Blues*
1948 *Swedish Pastry*
1950 *Sextet*
1954 *BG in Hi-fi*
1957 *Peggy Lee Sings with Benny Goodman*
1958 *Benny in Brussels, Vol. 1*
       Benny in Brussels, Vol. 2
1959 *In Stockholm 1959*
       The Benny Goodman Treasure Chest
1973 *The King Swings*
1998 *1935–1938*
       Portrait of Benny Goodman
              (Portrait Series)
       Carnegie Hall Jazz Concert '38
1999 *Bill Dodge All-star Recording*
       His Orchestra and His Combos
              (1941–1955)
       Live at Carnegie Hall

Chapter 1. An Overnight Success?

1. Ross Firestone, *Swing, Swing, Swing: The Life and Times of Benny Goodman* (New York: W.W. Norton & Company, 1993), p. 144.
2. Ibid.
3. Ibid., p. 145.
4. Ibid., p. 148.
5. Ibid., p. 149.

Chapter 2. Hard Times

1. Interview, *DownBeat,* February 8, 1956; quoted in "Benny Goodman Biography," retrieved July 8, 2011, http://www.lyricsfreak.com/b/benny+goodman/biography.html
2. Ross Firestone, *Swing, Swing, Swing: The Life and Times of Benny Goodman* (New York: W.W. Norton & Company, 1993), p. 19.
3. Benny Goodman and Irving Kolodin, *The Kingdom of Swing* (New York: Stackpole & Sons, 1939), p. 71.

Chapter 3. "The Kid in Short Pants"

1. Ross Firestone, *Swing, Swing, Swing: The Life and Times of Benny Goodman* (New York: W.W. Norton & Company, 1993), p. 25.
2. James Lincoln Collier, *Benny Goodman and the Swing Era* (New York: Oxford University Press, 1989), p. 52.
3. Firestone, p. 51.

Chapter 4. A Rocket Ride to Fame

1. Donald Clarke, *The Rise and Fall of Popular Music,* "The Swing Era Begins," *Donald Clarke's Music Box,* retrieved July 8, 2011, http://www.donaldclarkemusicbox.com/rise-and-fall/detail.php?c=10
2. Benny Goodman: Official Website of the King of Swing, "Quotes by Benny," retrieved June 30, 2011, http://www.bennygoodman.com/about/quotes.html
3. Ibid.
4. Firestone, p. 302.
5. James Lincoln Collier, *Benny Goodman and the Swing Era* (New York: Oxford University Press, 1989), p. 91.

6. Benny Goodman, "Quotes by Benny."
7. Firestone, p. 312.
8. *Jazz, a Film by Ken Burns.* Hollywood, California: Paramount Home Video and PBS Home Video, 2004.

Chapter 5. Beyond Swing
1. Ross Firestone, *Swing, Swing, Swing: The Life and Times of Benny Goodman* (New York: W.W. Norton & Company, 1993), p. 354.
2. Donald Clarke, *The Rise and Fall of Popular Music,* "The Swing Era Begins," *Donald Clarke's Music Box,* retrieved July 8, 2011, http://www.donaldclarkemusicbox.com/rise-and-fall/detail.php?c=10
3. Seymour "Sy" Brody, "Benny Goodman, the King of Swing," Florida Atlantic University Libraries, Jewish Heroes and Heroines in America, October 18, 2006, http://www.fau.edu/library/br123.htm
4. Benny Goodman: Official Website of the King of Swing, "Quotes by Benny," retrieved June 30, 2011, http://www.bennygoodman.com/about/quotes.html

BOOKS

While at the time of this printing there were no other books about Benny Goodman available for children, you might enjoy these other jazz musician books from Mitchell Lane Publishers:

Boone, Mary. *Dizzy Gillespie*. Hockessin, DE: Mitchell Lane Publishers, 2013.

Orr, Tamra. *Louis Armstrong*. Hockessin, DE: Mitchell Lane Publishers, 2013.

Rice, Earle, Jr. *Billie Holiday*. Hockessin, DE: Mitchell Lane Publishers, 2013.

Roberts, Russell. *Scott Joplin*. Hockessin, DE: Mitchell Lane Publishers, 2013.

Tracy, Kathleen. *Bessie Smith*. Hockessin, DE: Mitchell Lane Publishers, 2013.

WORKS CONSULTED

Benny Goodman: Official Website of the King of Swing. http://www.bennygoodman.com

Brody, Seymour "Sy." "Benny Goodman, The King of Swing." Florida Atlantic University Libraries, Jewish Heroes and Heroines in America, October 18, 2006. http://www.fau.edu/library/br123.htm

Clarke, Donald. *The Rise and Fall of Popular Music*. "The Swing Era Begins." *Donald Clarke's Music Box,* retrieved July 8, 2011. http://www.donaldclarkemusicbox.com/rise-and-fall/detail.php?c=10

Collier, James Lincoln. *Benny Goodman and the Swing Era*. New York: Oxford University Press, 1989.

Firestone, Ross. *Swing, Swing, Swing: The Life and Times of Benny Goodman*. New York: W.W. Norton & Company, Inc., 1993.

Goodman, Benny, and Irving Kolodin. *The Kingdom of Swing*. New York: Stackpole & Sons, 1939.

HyperMusic: A History of Jazz. http://www.hypermusic.ca/jazz/mainmenu.html

Jazz, a Film by Ken Burns. Hollywood, California: Paramount Home Video and PBS Home Video, 2004.

"PBS Jazz: Benny Goodman." http://www.pbs.org/jazz/biography/artist_id_goodman_benny.htm

Wilson, John S. "Benny Goodman, the King of Swing, Is Dead." *The New York Times,* June 14, 1986. http://www.nytimes.com/learning/general/onthisday/bday/0530.html

ON THE INTERNET

Jewish Heroes and Heroines of America. Florida Atlantic University Libraries.
http://www.fau.edu/library/bro3toc.htm

Making Music Fun. "Hey, Kids, Meet Benny Goodman."
http://www.makingmusicfun.net/htm/f_mmf_music_library/hey-kids-its-benny-goodman.htm

PBS Kids. "Jazz Greats: Benny Goodman."
http://pbskids.org/jazz/nowthen/goodman.html

Solid! "Benny Goodman Biography."
http://www.parabrisas.com/d_goodmanb.php

USA-Hero.com. "Benny Goodman Biography."
http://www.usa-hero.com/goodman_benny.html

PHOTO CREDITS: Cover—Joe Rasemas; pp. 4, 31—Bettman/Corbis; pp. 6, 22, 28, 29 (top), 35—Library of Congress; p. 10—AP Photo; pp. 13, 15, 19, 21, 29, 36, 37, 38—cc-by-sa; p. 16—Michael Ochs Archives/Getty Images; pp. 24, 25, 39—Frank Diggs Collection/Getty Images; p. 32—Herman Leonard; p. 34—March of Dimes; p. 37—Irving S. Gilmore Music Library/Benny Goodman Papers/Yale University. Every effort has been made to locate all copyright holders of material used in this book. If any errors or omissions have occurred, corrections will be made in future editions of the book.

arrangement (uh-RANJ-munt)—An adaptation of a musical composition so that it can be played by an orchestra.

collaborate (kuh-LAB-or-ayt)—To work together in order to create something.

duet (doo-ET)—A musical performance by two people.

embouchure (OM-buh-shur)—The position of the lips, tongue, and teeth when playing a wind or brass instrument.

gig (GIG)—A paid musical performance.

improvisation (im-prah-vuh-ZAY-shun)—The act of making up music on the spot, as it is performed.

jam session (JAM SEH-shun)—An informal performance by a group of musicians that often includes improvisation.

premiere (prih-MEER)—The first public performance; to be performed for the first time in public.

prodigy (PRAH-dih-jee)—Someone who displays exceptional talent at a young age.

publicist (PUB-lih-sist)—Someone who promotes or spreads news about a person, product, or event.

quartet (kwar-TET)—A group of four musicians playing together.

sextet (SEX-tet)—A group of six musicians playing together.

sideman (SYD-mun)—A member of a band or orchestra.

symphony (SIM-fuh-nee)—A long and complex piece of classical music.

trio (TREE-oh)—A group of three musicians playing together.

vibraphonist (VYE-bruh-foh-nist)—A musician who plays the vibraphone, a percussion instrument resembling a xylophone.

vocalist (VOH-kuh-list)—A singer.

About the Author

Joanne Mattern is the author of more than 200 nonfiction books for young readers. Her books for Mitchell Lane include biographies of notables such as Michelle Obama, Count Basie, Blake Lively, Selena, LeBron James, and Peyton Manning. Mattern grew up listening to big band, jazz, and popular music and thinks Benny Goodman's "Sing Sing Sing" is one of the best songs ever recorded. She also studied piano and voice for many years. She lives in New York State with her husband, four children, and an assortment of pets.